In and Out

Luana Mitten and Meg Greve

Rourke
Educational Media

rourkeeducationalmedia.com

www.rourkeeducationalmedia.com

PHOTO CREDITS: © Garrett Nudd: 3; © Nathan Jones: 4; © Anna Omeltchenko: 5; © Kevin Panizza: 6, 7; © Warwick Lister-Kaye: 8, 9; © Arpad Benedek: 10, 11; © Karoline Cullen: 12, 13; © Henry Fu: 14, 15; © NiseriN: 16, 17; © Chris Doyal: 18, 19; © Michael Galazka: 20, 21; © mrusty: 22; © stellajune3700: 23

Editor: Luana Mitten

Cover design by Nicola Stratford, bdpublishing.com

Interior Design by Tara Raymo

Library of Congress Cataloging-in-Publication Data

Mitten, Luana K.
In and out : concepts / Luana Mitten and Meg Greve.
   p. cm.
Includes bibliographical references and index.
ISBN 978-1-60694-383-0 (alk. paper) (hardcover)
ISBN 978-1-60694-515-5 (softcover)
ISBN 978-1-60694-573-5 (bilingual)
1. Space perception--Juvenile literature. I. Greve, Meg. II. Title.
BF469.M58 2010
423'.12--dc22
                                    2009016022
Rourke Educational Media
Printed in the United States of America,
North Mankato, Minnesota

rourkeeducationalmedia.com

customerservice@rourkeeducationalmedia.com • PO Box 643328 Vero Beach, Florida 32964

In and out, out and in,
what's the difference
between out and in?

I see the aquarium.
Let's go in!

4

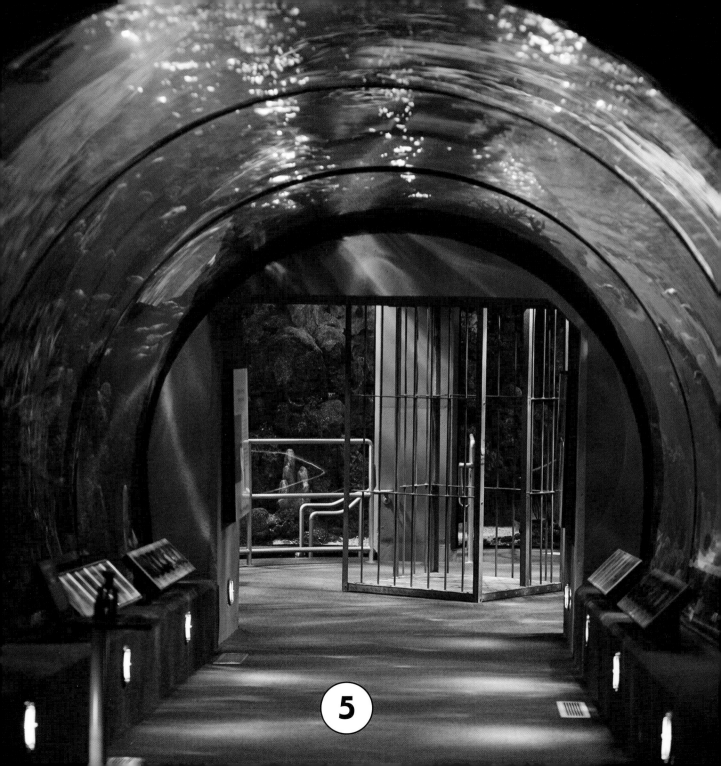

Sleepy eel in.
Shhhh.

Hungry eel out.
Careful!

Water goes in.

11

Water blows out.
Whoosh!

13

Dolphins jump out.

Dolphins dive in.
Splash!

16

Scared clownfish in.

18